ALPHABEEP
A Zipping, Zooming ABC

by Debora Pearson

illustrated by Edward Miller

Zipping, zooming down the street.... What's up ahead?
Come on— Beep, beep!

Aa is for Ambulance that makes alarming sounds. Shrieking, wailing, whooshing by, it's in a rush to help someone.

Bb is for Bulldozer. It crawls through muck, it clears out rubble. It moves big boulders as if they are pebbles.

Cc is for Cement Mixer.

In its belly, called the drum, wet cement flip-flops around then gushes out the chute.

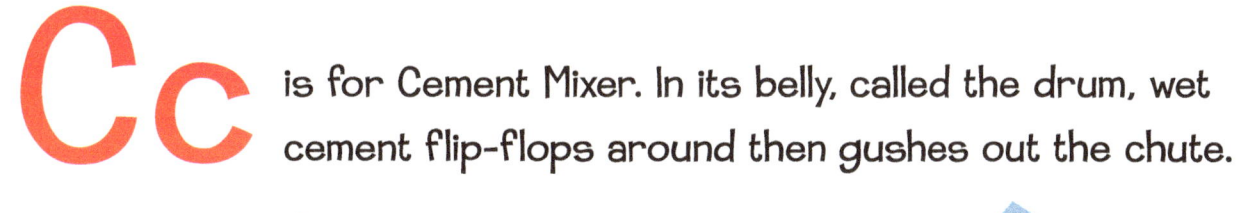

SIDEWALK CLOSED

PEBBLE'S CEMENT COMPANY

Dd is for Dump Truck. It thunders by with its load, stops and tips it on the ground. Clatter, crash, ka-Boom!

Ff is for Forklift that flits around the freight yard.
It lifts and lowers boxes with its long, steel fingers.

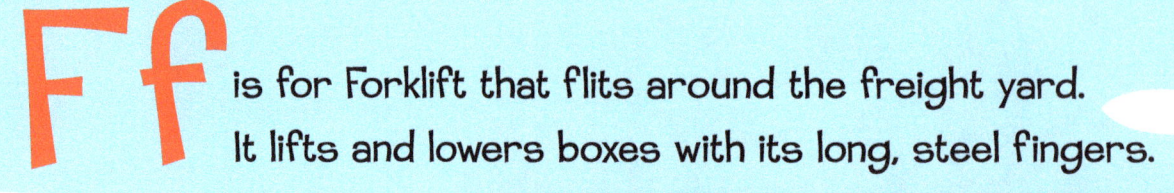

Gg is for Garbage Truck that growls along the road. It's on the prowl for stinky trash to squish, crunch, gr-r-r-r-rind.

Hh is for Hook and Ladder Truck. **Hurry, hurry**-race to the fire! Stretch out that ladder and douse those tall flames!

Ii is for Ice-Cream Truck, a chiming, tinkling, summertime truck. Buy a treat and lick it up—you'll feel cool instead of hot.

Jj is for Jeep. It bumps over fields, it splashes through streams. Jeeps don't need roads to get where they're going.

Kk is for Keep Left sign. Follow the arrow, go where it leads or you will hear... Honk! Screech! Beep, BEEP!

Mm is for Moving Truck. The space is immense at the back of this truck—it can hold EVERYTHING found in a house.

Nn
is for Newspaper Truck, always on the move. It zooms to newsstands and delivers the papers that people read each day.

Oo is for One Way sign. Big cars, little cars, fast and slow, all head in the same direction. Everyone goes with the flow.

Pp is for Police Car, speeding after bank robbers. In a flash, it howls past. Its mission? Catch those thieves!

Qq is for Quarry Excavator. It gnaws apart a tower of rubble, dropping rocks like crumbs. Its jaws can hold boulders as big as cars.

Rr is for Railroad Crossing sign. **Watch out, keep back**—trains roar along these tracks.

Ss

is for Street Cleaner. It scours the city in search of grime, scrubbing up dirt and devouring it.

Tt is for Tow Truck. It goes fishing for cars with its giant hook, reeling them up and dragging them off.

Uu is for Utility Truck that hoists a worker in its bucket. U-p... and u-p... the worker soars to fix the telephone wires.

Vv

is for Van, darting, dashing, zigzagging through traffic.
It's busy delivering packages—

vroooooom!

Ww is for Wrecking Crane. WHAM! When it swings its iron ball, buildings tumble to the ground.

Xx is for X-ray Truck that visits people who need X rays. It has a machine that takes pictures of the insides of their bodies.

Yy is for Yield sign. Take it easy, take it slow. Make way for other cars then go, go, go.

Zz is for Zamboni, finishing up its work. It shaves and cleans the ice, then covers it with water. When the water freezes, it becomes new ice to skate on.

Now the busy machine creeps off to its shed. The skaters have left, the rink is closed up—it's time to go to bed.

For my son,
Benjamin, my
enthusiastic guide
to the amazing world
of cars and trucks—D. P.

For my dad, who served as a traffic
cop for the NYC Police Department
for more than 20 years—E. M.

mhreadingwonders.com

Text copyright ©2004 by Debora Pearson.
Illustrations copyright ©2004 by Edward Miller.

Used by permission of Holiday House, Inc.

No part of this publication may be reproduced
or distributed in any form or by an means,
or stored in a database or retrieval system, without the
prior written consent of McGraw-Hill Education,
including, but not limited to, network storage or
transmission, or broadcast for distance learning.

Send all inquiries to:
McGraw-Hill Education
Two Penn Plaza
New York NY 10121
ISBN: 978-0-07-678370-0
MHID: 0-07-678370-7
Printed in Mexico
10 BRP 24